REVOLUTION AND CONFLICT

REVOLUTION AND CONFLICT

PETER
BEDRICK
BOOKS

This edition published in 2002 Peter Bedrick Books
an imprint of McGraw-Hill Children's Publishing
8787 Orion Place
Columbus, OH 43240

ISBN 1-57768-954-2

Printed in China

McGraw-Hill
Children's Publishing

A Division of The **McGraw·Hill** *Companies*

PHOTOGRAPHIC CREDITS

8 (B/R) CORBIS; 10 (C) Bettmann/CORBIS; 14 (C) Hulton-Deutsch Collection/CORBIS; 20 (C) Archivo
Iconografico, S.A./CORBIS; 23 (T/R) Museum of the City of New York/CORBIS; 31 (T/R) CORBIS; 37
(T/L) Minnesota Historical Society/CORBIS; 39 (T/R) Bettmann/CORBIS; 40 (C) Hulton-Deutsch
Collection/CORBIS; 42 (B/R) CORBIS; 43 (T/R) Bettmann/CORBIS. All other images from the Miles Kelly
Archive.

QUOTATION ACKNOWLEDGEMENTS

Pages 7, 15, 21, 33, 37, 41, 47 published in the *Oxford Dictionary of Quotations* by the Oxford University Press;
page 11 quoted in *World Book Encyclopedia*, published by World Book, Inc.

Every effort has been made to trace all copyright holders and obtain permissions. The editor and publishers sincere-
ly apologise for any inadvertent errors or omissions and will be happy to correct them in any future editions.

Contents

AD

By the 1760s, explorers had traveled far enough to give map makers a rough idea of the shape of the world. But one enormous mystery remained – the Pacific Ocean. No one knew how big it was or how many islands it contained.

Discovering Australia

Many believed that there must be a large continent somewhere in the southern seas, waiting to be discovered. Seamen such as Abel Tasman and William Dampier had reached the coasts of Australia and New Zealand but had thought they were just small islands. Few wanted to venture farther. The southern Pacific is a dangerous place, with typhoons and swirling currents.

Willem Jancz is the first European to sight the Australian coast.	1606
Abel Tasman gains first sight of the island named after him – Tasmania.	1642
James Cook charts the coast of New Zealand's North and South islands.	1769
Cook explores and lands on Australia's east coast.	1770
Britain establishes first convict colony at Botany Bay.	1788
Traders and whale hunters begin regular visits to New Zealand waters.	c. 1790
Flinders sails right round Australia, proving it to be a single huge island.	1801–1803
Western Australia claimed for Britain by Charles Fremantle.	1829

Cook and the *Endeavour*

In 1768, the British government sent an expedition to find the mysterious southern continent. Its leader was James Cook, and his ship was a small but tough vessel called *Endeavour*. After visiting the island of Tahiti, Cook sailed southward, then west until he sighted an unknown land. It turned out to be New Zealand.

Landfall in Australia

The Endeavour sailed on, searching for the east coast of Australia. Previous explorers had spotted Tasmania and the rocky western shore, but no European had yet landed on the east side. At last, Cook reached the coast of what he knew to be Australia.

△ Cook's first meeting with the Maori people of New Zealand took place in 1769. With great care, Cook made a voyage lasting six months around both the North and South islands of New Zealand. Charting the coastline as he sailed, Cook soon realized that he had not found a vast continent.

△ In 1776, Cook set sail to find a sea passage from the Pacific around the north of America to the Atlantic. Ice blocked his way. He was the first European to reach Hawaii, where he was killed in 1779.

Scientific work

On board the *Endeavour* was a group of scientists whose task was to record the animals and plants they saw on the voyage. The name of Botany Bay was chosen because of the unusual plants the scientists saw on its shores.

He followed it northward until he found a suitable place to land. He called this Botany Bay.

Later voyages

A year later, in 1772, Cook set out again from England for the Pacific. Although Australia seemed big, it was not big enough to be the new continent. This time, Cook had to explore all of the southern ocean. His great voyage took him as far as the pack ice inside the Antarctic Circle and around the globe. It proved that there was no vast continent in the south.

Convicts and settlers

James Cook had opened up the Pacific region to later explorers and settlers. He had also claimed Australia as a British possession. His government decided to use this seemingly wild and empty land as a punishment colony for criminals. The first shiploads of convicts and their guards landed at Botany Bay in 1788.

More convicts and settlers arrived in the early 1800s, forcing the native Aboriginals to leave large areas of their tribal lands. Many fell victim to European diseases. It was the same in New Zealand, where the Maoris were helpless against Western firearms and germs.

[My aim was] not only to go farther than anyone had done before but as far as possible for man to go.
CAPTAIN JAMES COOK (1728–1779)

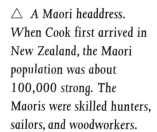

△ A Maori headdress. When Cook first arrived in New Zealand, the Maori population was about 100,000 strong. The Maoris were skilled hunters, sailors, and woodworkers.

AD

The Seven Years' War saw the end of French power in North America. By 1763, more than two million British colonists were living there. Now they wanted to be able to govern themselves. Britain, however, had different ideas about her colonies, because they were an important market for trade.

American Revolution

A large British army and naval fleet was still stationed to protect North America. The British government was concerned about who was going to pay for these forces. The answer was the colonists themselves – through new and increased taxes.

Protest and rebellion

The British government imposed several new taxes, on things as different as official paper and molasses. The Americans had never been taxed before and protested loudly. Some of the taxes were removed, but import duties on luxury goods such as tea were increased.

The Americans had no one to put their case democratically to the parliament in London, so they took direct action. At the famous

Britain imposes Stamp Act on the colonies.	1765
Many taxes removed but not the tax on tea.	1770
Boston Tea Party sparks rebellion throughout Massachusetts.	1773
First battles at Concord and Lexington lead to war.	1775
The American Declaration of Independence.	1776
American victory at Saratoga.	1777
France enters the war on the American side.	1778
Cornwallis surrenders at Yorktown.	1781
Treaty of Versailles grants independence to the United States.	1783

△ The American victory over British forces at Saratoga in 1777 was a turning point in the war. Surrounded on all sides and outnumbered, the British were forced to surrender.

▷ In 1773, a band of colonists seized three British ships in Boston harbor and dumped their cargo of tea overboard. This incident became known as the "Boston Tea Party." It enraged the British government, who sent troops to put Massachusetts under military rule.

"Boston Tea Party" the colonists dumped the cargo of tea from three British ships into Boston harbor.

War begins

By 1775, the whole colony was in a state of rebellion. The British commander learned that Americans were stockpiling ammunition at the village of Concord, and they sent soldiers to destroy it. The resulting battle, and another at nearby Lexington, marked the opening of America's struggle for freedom.

The war went badly for Britain from the start. A force was sent to cut off New England from the other colonies in 1777, but it was defeated at the battle of Saratoga. In 1778, the Americans gained new allies when the French declared war on Britain and sent troops and ships across the Atlantic, attacking settlements in the West Indies.

△ In 1775, George Washington was elected as commander-in-chief of the colonists' army. To many Americans at that time, he became a leading symbol of their fight for independence.

Surrender at Yorktown

In 1780, British troops, led by Lord Cornwallis, captured the town of Charleston and defeated the colonists at Camden. Once again the British forces were cut off, and in October 1781, Cornwallis was forced to surrender at Yorktown. The war was over.

Declaration of Independence

On July 4, 1776, representatives of the 13 colonies signed the Declaration of Independence. This broke off all political connections with Britain, abandoned loyalty to the British monarchy, and created the United States of America. Thomas Jefferson, one of the lawyers who helped to draw up the declaration, later became president of the United States.

△ The American flag, which later became known as the Stars and Stripes, was first flown at the battle of Bennington in 1777. The 13 red and white stripes, and the 13 stars, stood for the 13 original colonies that signed the Declaration of Independence. The modern American flag has 50 stars, one for each state.

Victory in the American Revolution had freed the 13 colonies from British rule. They now controlled all of North America between the Mississippi River and the Atlantic, apart from British Canada and Spanish Florida. Their next task was to organize themselves into a nation.

The Birth of the U.S.

In 1787, American leaders (the "Founding Fathers") wrote a constitution for the United States, which became the basis of all the country's laws. They also set up a government and chose George Washington to be their very first president.

The Founding Fathers write the Constitution.	1787
George Washington becomes the first president.	1789
The Louisiana Purchase.	1803
Tecumseh leads Creek Indians against the white settlers in southern USA.	1813
The Indian Removal Act is passed.	1830
US war against Mexico to secure Texas and Oregon.	1846–1848
Gold Rush to California begins.	1848
War against the Sioux tribes of the Plains.	1854–1890
War against the Apache in the far south.	1861–1900

The Louisiana Purchase

Weakened by war, Spain had given up its hold in North America. The French took over a large area of territory called Louisiana, stretching from west of the Mississippi across to the Rocky Mountains. But France also had a European war to cope with, and in 1803, France sold Louisiana to the United States government. The Louisiana Purchase doubled the size of the country.

Into the west

By 1820, the United States had grown even larger. It took over the Red River Basin from Britain and gained possession of Florida from Spain. Already settlers were pouring westward into the new territory, founding communities by the Mississippi, then spreading beyond it into Missouri and Texas. Thousands of settlers cleared land in order to build farms and houses. They were followed by a steady stream of traders, manufacturers, doctors, and teachers, and soon the first frontier towns were forming.

△ In 1803, an exploration party set out to discover what the northwest territory was like. Led by Meriwether Lewis and William Clark, the party crossed the Rockies to the Pacific coast and brought back important news about the region.

△ *The Native Americans stood little chance against the powerful firearms and huge numbers of the settlers. They were defeated in a series of bitter wars during the 1700s.*

Thomas Jefferson

Thomas Jefferson was the third president of the United States. A serious political thinker, he wrote the Declaration of Independence. His handbook of rules for the US Senate is still in use today.

War with Mexico

Many Americans believed that the United States should govern all of North America. But large areas, including most of Oregon and Texas, were still under the control of Mexico. As white settlers pushed into these territories, there was bound to be trouble.

By 1836, the settlers had taken over most of eastern Texas and declared it an independent country. The United States government took over the region in 1845 and a year later moved into Oregon. The war against a weak Mexican army was short and one-sided. In 1848, the Mexicans gave in and signed a peace treaty, granting the United States the land stretching from the Gulf of Mexico to the Pacific coast. This almost doubled the country's size once again.

Native Americans

As the settlers flooded west, they invaded the ancient tribal lands of the Native Americans. Alarmed at losing their hunting grounds, the Native Americans began to fight the newcomers. In 1830, the government allowed troops to move the tribes to empty land beyond the Mississippi. From about 1850 to 1890, the tribes who lived on the Great Plains were gradually conquered or wiped out. Survivors were confined to "reservations" on land that the settlers did not want.

'Tis our true policy to steer clear of permanent Alliances, with any portion of the foreign world. There can be no greater error than to expect favours from nation to nation.
GEORGE WASHINGTON'S FAREWELL ADDRESS, 1796

△ *As new lands opened up, railroads were built to carry settlers and supplies to the west more quickly. The Union Pacific Railroad, linking the east and west coasts, opened in 1869.*

In 1789, the people of France overthrew their monarchy in the name of liberty and equality. This was the start of the French Revolution. The events of the revolution eventually sparked off a whole series of wars in Europe that lasted until 1815, when the French emperor, Napoleon Bonaparte, was finally defeated and sent into exile.

Power and Rights

Liberty was also the cry in South America, as colonies under the control of Spain and Portugal began to demand their independence. The main leaders in the fight for independence were the Venezuelan, Simon Bolívar, and the Argentine, José de San Martín. By 1830, the countries of South America were free of foreign rule.

In Europe, too, there were battles for independence. The *Risorgimento* is the name given to the movement for Italian unification. The kingdom of Italy was formed in 1861, and Rome became the capital of the newly united country ten years later. In that same year, the first *kaiser* (emperor) of a united Germany was crowned.

Trade wars

The 1800s was a time of European power, when many nations began to establish new overseas empires. In Britain, and later in France, Russia, and Germany, the Industrial Revolution encouraged the search for new sources of inexpensive raw materials and new markets for manufactured goods. Britain expanded its control in India, and white exploration began to open up the continent of Africa to European exploitation. In the Far East, Britain and the U.S. forced both China and Japan to open their markets to foreign trade.

Slave wars

In the U.S. conflict over the issue of slavery led to a bitter civil war between the northern and southern states. Slavery was finally abolished, but at the end of the war, much of the South lay in ruins. The country expanded westward, as pioneer families continued to try their luck on farms in California, Oregon, and on the Great Plains. As white settlers moved into these areas, the Native Americans were forced off lands that had been their home for generations.

AD

At the end of the Seven Years' War, France lost its colonies in America and India to Britain. In retaliation, French troops fought alongside American colonists in the American War of Independence. The cost of these wars left France virtually bankrupt.

Revolution in France

To try to raise money, the French king, Louis XVI, proposed an increase in taxes. However, most of the country's richest people – the clergy (known as the First Estate) and the noblemen (the Second Estate) – did not pay tax. So the burden of taxes fell on the ordinary people – the peasants and middle classes (known as the Third Estate).

A population boom meant that there was too little food for too many people. The noblemen and clergy refused to change the law on taxes, so the king called a meeting of all three states – the Estates-General.

Events of 1789

The Estates-General met at the Palace of Versailles in May 1789. The meeting coincided with unrest in France, as harvests in 1788 had failed and many people were facing starvation. Still, the first two estates refused to let the Third Estate have a say in governing the country. The Third Estate formed a national assembly and vowed not to disperse until government was reformed in France. Louis appeared to give in – at the same time gathering troops to break up the assembly.

Harvests fail in France.	1788
Estates-General meet in May. Declaration of Rights of Man and of the Citizen.	1789
Crowds attack Bastille Prison in Paris (July 14). French Revolution begins.	1789
Royal family tries unsuccessfully to escape.	1791
France goes to war against Austria and Prussia. France is declared a republic.	1792
Louis XVI is executed on the guillotine. "Reign of Terror" starts.	1793
"Reign of Terror" ends with execution of Robespierre.	1794
Napoleon seizes control of government.	1799

△ On July 14, 1789, a mob attacked the royal prison in Paris, the Bastille. Although only a few prisoners were released, this event marked the end of royal power in France and the beginning of the Revolution. Bastille Day is still celebrated as a national holiday in France each year on July 14.

△ Queen Marie Antoinette, wife of Louis XVI. Her forceful personality enabled her to influence the weak-minded king. Although beautiful, Marie Antoinette was unpopular with ordinary French people because of her extravagant spending.

The guillotine

A French doctor, a member of France's National Assembly, suggested the use of the guillotine as an instrument of execution. He recommended it as a quick and painless way to behead people.

As rumors multiplied and food supplies worsened, panic began to spread. When a Paris mob stormed the Bastille prison in Paris in July, the power of the monarchy was seriously weakened, and the Revolution had begun. In August, the National Assembly issued a Declaration of the Rights of Man, stating that all citizens were free and equal and had the right to resist oppression.

The French Republic

Louis XVI remained opposed to the National Assembly's reforms, refusing to share power with the new government. In 1792, France went to war against Austria and Prussia. The revolutionaries accused the king and his aristocratic friends of helping the enemy, and in August, the king and his family were imprisoned. In September, the monarchy was abolished, and France was declared a republic.

Louis XVI was tried for betraying his country and beheaded. This period was known as the "Reign of Terror," when thousands of people suspected of plotting against the government were killed. In these troubled times, French armies continued to repel their enemies, due partly to a military leader named Napoleon Bonaparte. In 1799, he seized power from the government — the revolution had ended.

Liberté Egalité Fraternité

△ The new French Republic adopted as its official slogan the words "Liberté, Egalité, Fraternité" [which means liberty, equality, fraternity (brotherhood)].

" Any law which violates the indefensible rights of man is essentially unjust and tyrannical; it is not a law at all.
MAXIMILIEN ROBESPIERRE, 24 APRIL, 1793

Robespierre was one of the leaders of the Revolution.

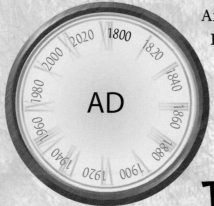

AD

After years of political dispute and unrest, the French people welcomed Napoleon as their new leader in 1799. Not only was Napoleon a brilliant general, he also proved himself to be a skillful administrator. He reorganized the administration of France, dividing the country into regions called departments.

The Napoleonic Wars

Napoleon ordered the reorganization of French law into codes. The *Code Napoléon* still forms the basis for part of French law today. In 1804, the French people voted for Napoleon to be emperor of France. He crowned himself emperor at Notre Dame Cathedral at the end of that year.

To war

Although Europe was at peace briefly in 1802, Napoleon's thoughts soon turned to extending French control and building an empire. To raise money, he sold a large area of land in North America, called Louisiana, to the Americans. In 1803, France and Britain went to war again. Napoleon wanted to land an army in Britain, so he needed to control the seas. But in 1805, a British fleet under Lord Nelson defeated the combined French and Spanish fleets at the battle of Trafalgar. This defeat ended Napoleon's hopes of invading Britain.

Treaty of Amiens brings peace between France and Britain.	1802
Napoleon sells Louisiana territory to United States to raise money for war.	1803
Britain and France go to war once again.	1803
Napoleon crowns himself emperor.	1804
British destroy French and Spanish fleets at battle of Trafalgar.	1805
Napoleon's army wins at Ulm and Austerlitz.	1805
Start of Peninsular War in Spain and Portugal.	1808
French troops are defeated by bitter Russian winter.	1812
Napoleon exiled in Elba. He returns to be defeated at Waterloo.	1815

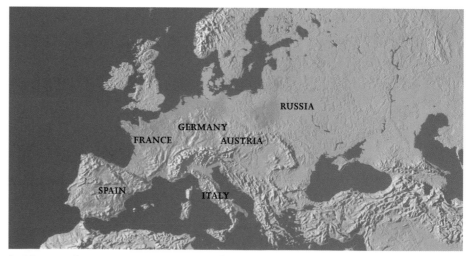

△ The French Empire under Napoleon. After abandoning attempts to increase French influence in North America, Napoleon's attention turned to expanding his empire in Europe.

▷ The combined armies of Britain, Austria, Prussia, and Russia defeated Napoleon's army at the battle of Waterloo in 1815. It was to be Napoleon's last battle. The French had more soldiers and better artillery but they were still soundly beaten.

△ Napoleon is considered to be a great military genius and one of the greatest commanders in history. Yet he was also described as an "enemy and disturber of the peace of the world."

In 1805, Russia, Austria, and Sweden joined Britain in a coalition against France. But Napoleon's massive armies won major victories at battles such as Ulm (against the Austrians) and Austerlitz (against the Russians). In 1806, Napoleon decided to blockade the transport of British goods. Any ship that entered a French-controlled port after calling at a British port was seized by the French authorities. However, this policy disrupted trade across Europe and made Napoleon very unpopular. Neither was it very successful, as Britain continued to expand trade with its overseas colonies.

End of the empire

By 1812, Napoleon had created a French empire that covered almost all of Europe. However, after a disastrous campaign in Russia, Napoleon's empire began to crumble. In April 1814, Napoleon was forced to abdicate. He went into exile in Elba, an island off the coast of Italy, only to return with fresh troops the following year to make another bid for power. Napoleon's final defeat came at the battle of Waterloo in June 1815. He was sent into exile on the island of St. Helena in the South Atlantic Ocean, where he died in 1821.

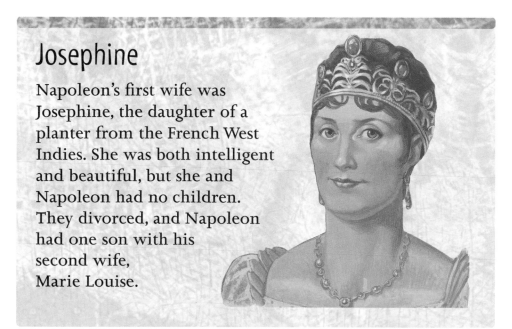

Josephine

Napoleon's first wife was Josephine, the daughter of a planter from the French West Indies. She was both intelligent and beautiful, but she and Napoleon had no children. They divorced, and Napoleon had one son with his second wife, Marie Louise.

△ Napoleon's distinctive hat. Napoleon was a great military strategist, who seemed instinctively to know the best time to attack during a battle. But his campaign in Russia during the winter of 1812 was disastrous, ending without victory and with the death or capture of about 500,000 French soldiers.

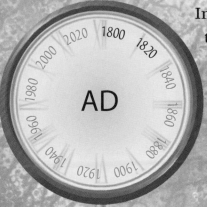

AD

In the early 1800s, colonies in South America under the control of Spain and Portugal began to demand their independence. The main leaders in the struggle against Spanish rule were the Venezuelan, Simon Bolívar, and the Argentine, José de San Martín.

Struggles in South America

Bolívar was born into a wealthy family and was sent to Europe to complete his education. It was in Rome in 1804 that Bolívar made a vow to liberate his country. Taking advantage of the weakening of Spanish authority caused by the Napoleonic Wars, Venezuela declared its independence from Spain in 1811. But the Spaniards retained control of the country, and it took another ten years of fighting before Venezuela became truly free from colonial rule.

Venezuela declares independence.	1811
José de San Martín leads fight for *Argentine* independence from Spain.	1812
Argentina becomes independent.	1816
Chile becomes independent from Spain after battle of Chacabuco.	1818
Bolívar leads troops to victory against Spanish at battle of Boyacá.	1819
San Martín leads army into Peru.	1820
San Martín proclaims independence of Peru.	1821
Venezuela becomes truly independent after battle of Carabobo.	1821
Bolivia named after Simon Bolívar.	1825

Simon Bolívar

The turning point came in 1819 when Bolívar and his small army surprised the Spanish in the colony of New Granada (present-day Colombia). He mounted an attack on them at the battle of Boyacá. After this resounding victory, Bolívar set up the Republic of Gran Colombia.

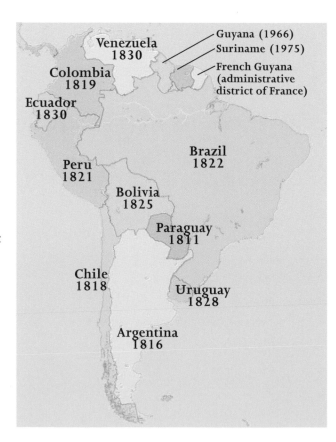

▷ The struggles for independence in South America began in the early 1800s. One by one, the countries freed themselves from foreign rule. The dates shown are when each country gained its independence.

▷ Caracas is the capital city of Venezuela and is the birthplace of Simon Bolívar. The revolutionary leader made a triumphant entrance into the city in June 1821 after the battle of Carabobo.

△ Simon Bolívar was known as el Libertador (the Liberator). He was a great general and military leader who was inspired by the ideal that all people should be equal and free.

It included the present-day countries of Colombia, Venezuela, and Ecuador. In 1821, Bolívar finally took control of the Venezuelan capital, Caracas, after the battle of Carabobo.

José de San Martín

In the southern part of the continent, a similar process was happening under the leadership of San Martín. He was an army officer who had fought in the Spanish army against French invaders in the Napoleonic Wars. But in 1811, San Martín decided to return home and join the fight for independence. Argentina declared its independence in 1812. San Martín then joined forces with a freedom fighter from Chile, Bernardo O'Higgins. Together, they led a force across the Andes Mountains and surprised the Spanish at the battle of Chacabuco. Chilean independence followed in 1818.

Only Peru remained under Spanish rule. In 1820, San Martín led an army into Peru, and in the following year, he proclaimed independence. But a small stronghold of Spanish troops remained. In 1822, San Martín requested assistance from Bolívar, and it was left to Bolívar's armies to liberate the last regions in South America from Spanish rule. Bolivia was named in Bolívar's honor in 1825.

José de San Martín

San Martín is one of the greatest heroes of modern Argentina. After joining forces with Bernardo O'Higgins and defeating the Spanish at Chacabuco in 1817, San Martín went on to win another victory – at Maipú in northern Chile – the following year.

△ The fighting in South America ended about 300 years of colonial rule by five nations in Europe – Portugal, Spain, Britain, Holland, and France.

AD

The Crimean War was fought in the Crimean Peninsula (in present-day Ukraine) between Russia and the allied armies of Britain, France, the Ottoman Empire (Turkey), and Sardinia-Piedmont. The war was a result of religious conflicts between Russia and the Ottoman Empire.

Conflict in Europe

Russia invades Turkish provinces. Turkey declares war on Russia.	1853
British and French forces land in the Crimea.	1854
Battles of Alma (September), Balaklava (October), Inkerman (November).	1854
Treaty of Paris ends Crimean War.	1856
Guiseppe Garibaldi and army of "red shirts"' start revolt in Sicily.	1860
Victor-Emmanuel II becomes king of Italy.	1861
Franco-Prussian War ends with crowning of Wilhelm as emperor of Germany.	1870–1871
Rome captured and made capital of unified Italy.	1871

The governments of Britain and France were particularly concerned about Russia's intentions to expand its territories. In 1853, Russia invaded Turkish provinces on the River Danube and declared war on the Ottoman Empire.

When Russian ships destroyed part of the Turkish fleet, Britain and France declared war on Russia. In order to avoid the threat of Austria joining the alliance against it, Russia withdrew from the Danube provinces in the summer of 1854. Austria then occupied these provinces.

British and French forces landed on the Crimea in 1854. The aim was to launch a swift attack on the Russian fortress of Sevastopol. Instead, the campaign to take the fortress turned from a swift and decisive victory into a year-long siege in which many thousands of soldiers on both sides lost their lives. Eventually, Russia finally agreed to sign a peace treaty in March 1856.

The unification of Italy
The Treaty of Paris that brought the Crimean War to an end did little to bring stability to Europe. The leader

△ In 1860, Guiseppe Garibaldi, having returned from exile, led his army of "red shirts" in a revolt that started on the island of Sicily. Having conquered the Kingdom of the Two Sicilies, Garibaldi and his army of 1,000 volunteeers then went on to take the city of Naples.

△ Paris in 1848, the so-called "year of revolutions" when unrest and rebellion broke out in many European countries. In Paris, people took to the streets to demand a new republic as well as votes for all males. Government soldiers shot and killed some of the rioters.

Florence Nightingale

Florence Nightingale was an English nurse who organized the care of wounded British soldiers in the Crimea. In 1854, she sailed to the Crimea with 38 nurses. She introduced many reforms and raised nursing standards.

of Sardinia-Piedmont, Count Cavour, used the meetings at Paris to demand unification for Italy. At that time, Italy was made up of many separate states, most controlled by Austria. Sardinia-Piedmont was the only independent state.

The movement for independence, known as the Risorgimento, started in the 1820s and 1830s. In 1858, Sardinia-Piedmont allied itself with France and drove out the Austrians from much of northern Italy. The successful revolt by Guiseppe Garibaldi and his "red shirts" led eventually to the unification of all of Italy. Italy was declared a kingdom under King Victor-Emmanuel II in 1861. Rome was captured and made the capital of a unified Italy in 1871.

The unification of Germany

After the Napoleonic Wars, Germany's many small states were joined to form the German Confederation. Of the 39 states in the Confederation, Austria, and Prussia were the most powerful. In 1862, King Wilhelm of Prussia appointed Otto von Bismarck as his prime minister. Bismarck masterminded three wars which allowed Prussia to extend German territory, seize control from Austria, and take the region of Alsace-Lorraine from France. In 1871, Wilhelm was crowned the first *kaiser* (emperor) of a united Germany.

"Anyone who wants to carry on the war ... come with me. I can't offer you either honors or wages; I offer you hunger, thirst, forced marches, battles and death.
GUISEPPE GARIBALDI, 1882

△ Florence Nightingale was known as the "Lady with the Lamp" because of the light she carried at night. She would walk through the hospital corridors, checking on her patients.

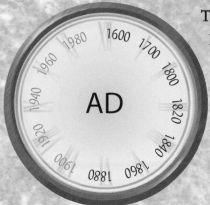

AD

Throughout history, travel had been a problem. Roads were poor, often muddy and full of holes (one traveler actually drowned in a pothole in 17th-century England). Transport depended on muscle power – people on two legs or horses and mules on four.

Travel and Transport

Heavy goods could go more swiftly by sea, but there were always the dangers of storms and pirates. The Industrial Revolution, which began in Europe in the early 1700s, saw dramatic improvements in travel and the carrying of cargo.

Better roads

In Britain, private roads called turnpikes were built in the 1750s, and travelers had to pay tolls to use them. But these soon became rutted and in need of repair. In about 1810, a Scottish engineer called John Macadam developed a new type of hard-wearing road surface that drained easily. It consisted of a thick layer of stones covered with gravel and rubble. Another Scot, Thomas Telford, built roads with a foundation of large flat stones, helping to make travel smoother and faster.

By river and canal

People had always used rivers for carrying freight. Pulling a barge, a horse could haul a load 30 times heavier than the one it could haul by road. As industry expanded, greater loads of heavy goods such as coal

Canal du Midi completed in France.	1681
First major canal built in England – the Grand Trunk Canal.	1777
Trevithick builds steam locomotive Catch-me-who-can.	1804
Fulton tests first successful steamboat.	1807
Macadam develops new type of road surface.	1810
Erie Canal opens.	1825
Brunel begins building the Great Western Railway.	1835
Atlantic steamship Great Western launched.	1837
Union Pacific Railway links east and west coasts of U.S.	1869

▷ Scottish engineer Thomas Telford was most famous for building bridges. From 1792, he designed over 1,200 bridges for roads and railways, such as the Menai Bridge, shown here.

▷ *A painting of the Erie Canal in the northeast United States. Its first section was completed in 1820. The canal allowed ships to travel from the Atlantic Ocean to the Great Lakes.*

and iron had to be taken across country. Rivers did not always go in the right direction, so canals were dug instead. The first modern canal system opened in France in 1681 and was later copied in Britain and the U.S. By about 1800, there were nearly 4,400 miles of canal in Britain.

Steam power

Steam power was the driving force of the Industrial Revolution. But early steam engines were too heavy to move themselves around. It was only in 1804 that the Englishman Richard Trevithick built a steam engine which could move itself along iron rails. His idea was developed by George Stephenson, whose locomotive *Rocket* was used to pull trains from 1829. For the first time, people could travel faster than a galloping horse. Trains could also carry large cargoes of raw materials to industrial centers and food to the growing towns.

Steam was also being used to power ships. In 1807, Robert Fulton built the first financially successful steamboat. Then, in 1837, English engineer Isambard Kingdom Brunel launched the *Great Western*, the first all-steam ship to carry passengers across the Atlantic.

△ *American Robert Fulton built the first successful steamboat, the* Clermont, *in 1807. It operated passenger services on the Hudson River. Soon paddlesteamers were at work on rivers and channels across the U.S. and Europe.*

Washington

Brunel's massive ship the *Great Eastern* had screw propellers as well as paddlewheels. The success of the *Great Eastern* inspired ship builders in Europe and the U.S. to invest in steam powered ships. The USS *Washington* is one such example.

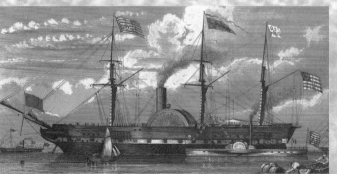

△ *A paddlewheel from Brunel's* Great Eastern, *launched in 1843. The iron-built vessel was the model for today's ocean-going ships.*

23

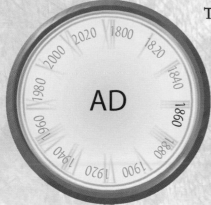

AD

The American Civil War (1861–1865) was fought between the northern (Union) states and the southern (Confederate) states. The differences between the two arose mainly from the question of slavery.

The American Civil War

The economy of the southern states was based on large plantations growing tobacco and cotton, using slave labor. The economy of the northern states was based on smaller farms and manufacturing. Many people in the North were appalled by the continued use of slave labor in the U.S.

Abraham Lincoln becomes president. Southern states withdraw from the Union.	1860
Six southern states form the Confederacy.	1861
First battle of the American Civil War at Fort Sumter.	1861
First battle between iron-clad ships the Virginia and Monitor.	1862
Emancipation Proclamation. Battle of Gettysburg.	1863
Union armies destroy large portion of southern states.	1864
Civil War ends. Abolition of slavery becomes law in the 13th Amendment.	1865

Slave labor

Around 4 million slaves worked in the southern states, accounting for almost one-third of the south's population. The northern states wanted to ensure that slavery would be banned in any new states admitted to the Union. By the 1850s, many had begun to call for the complete abolition of slavery. The southern states threatened to leave the Union if this abolition was imposed on them.

△ The battle over Fort Sumter in Charleston Harbor, South Carolina, marked the beginning of the American Civil War. Confederate soldiers fired on the Union troops

24

△ Robert E. Lee, commander of the Confederate forces, was a clever general and a skilled military planner.

△ Abraham Lincoln was assassinated by a Confederate sympathizer in 1865, five days after the surrender of General Lee and the Confederate forces.

△ Black slaves working on a cotton plantation in the South. Southerners argued that they needed the slaves to keep the South's economy going.

Union and Confederate states

The United States was split into two halves by the Civil War. In the north were the states of the Union; in the south were the 11 states that broke away and formed the Confederacy. The war killed more Americans than any other war.

Union states

Confederate states

Union states containing Confederate supporters

President Lincoln

In 1860, Abraham Lincoln was elected president of the United States. He was against slavery, and his election convinced the leaders of the southern states that the only choice they had was to leave the Union. South Carolina was the first state to secede (leave) in 1860, soon followed by Mississippi, Florida, Alabama, Georgia, and Louisiana. These states formed the Confederate States of America in 1861. The northern states were determined to preserve the Union, if necessary by force. The first shots were fired at Fort Sumter in South Carolina on April 12, 1861.

A bloody war

Large armies were quickly raised on both sides, and thousands of black soldiers became Union troops. The Confederate armies were commanded by General Robert E. Lee; the Union commander was General Ulysses S. Grant. At first, the Confederate armies were victorious, but a turning-point came at the battle of Gettysburg in 1863, after which Union armies pushed the southerners back into Virginia. In the same year, President Lincoln abolished slavery throughout the United States – a measure that became law in 1865.

In 1864, Union armies destroyed large areas of the South in a final effort to break the will of the Confederate states. When the war finally came to an end in 1865, slavery had been abolished and the Union preserved. But thousands of people had died, many from disease, and large areas of the United States lay in ruins.

△ The Confederates' battle flag. It had 13 stars – 11 for the states of the Confederacy and one each for Kentucky and Missouri, which did not secede.

For 700 years, Japan was under the rule of the Japanese military leaders known as shoguns. The shoguns had been careful to control European influence in Japan. In the 1600s, Christian missionaries were banned from the country and, after 1639, only Dutch ships were allowed into Japanese waters to trade.

Emergence of Japan

In the 19th century, the United States and several European countries forced Japan to open up to world trade. In 1853, American warships sailed into Edo Bay under the command of Commodore Matthew Perry. Perry delivered a letter requesting trade and diplomatic relations with Japan. He returned the following year for an answer, and the shogun had little choice but to sign a trade treaty with the United States. This was soon followed by treaties with Britain, France, the Netherlands, and Russia.

American warships sail into Edo Bay under command of Commodore Matthew Perry.	1853
Trade agreements signed between Japan and U.S.	1854
More trade agreements between Japan, U.S., Britain, the Netherlands, Russia.	1858
"Meiji restoration" — return of imperial rule.	1868
Iwakura mission tours Europe and North America.	1872
Chinese-Japanese war. Taiwan becomes a Japanese province.	1894–1895
War between Japan and Russia.	1904–1905
Korea becomes a Japanese territory.	1910
End of Meiji era.	1912

The Meiji restoration

The 1860s was a time of uncertainty and political unrest in Japan. Finally, in 1868, the situation became so serious that Emperor Mutsuhito took control from the last shogun. Mutsuhito became known as the Meiji emperor, and this event is called the "Meiji restoration."
Under the emperor's authority, Japan embarked on

▷ *During the period of Meiji rule, education was introduced for all Japanese people. The Meiji emperor also gave farmers ownership of their land and changed Japan's army and navy into modern military forces.*

▷ The modern city of Tokyo, the capital and largest city in Japan. Emperor Mutsuhito moved Japan's capital in 1868 from Kyoto to Edo, then renamed the city Tokyo.

△ Commodore Perry and his fleet of warships sailed into Edo Bay on July 8, 1853. He handed over the United States' demands for setting up trade and diplomatic relations with Japan.

a program of modernization. In 1872, a group of Japanese politicians went on a tour of Europe and North America to learn more about industry, education, and ways of life in the West.

As a result, factories were built in Japan, and the country began to change from an agricultural to an industrialized nation. A railway network was constructed, the Bank of Japan opened, and new education systems were put in place. The unfair treaties that had been signed in 1858 were renegotiated in the 1890s, with better terms for Japan.

Japan at war

Japan also built up its armed forces and went to war to acquire colonies of its own. In 1895, Taiwan became a Japanese province following a war with China. In 1904, Japan captured Port Arthur, destroyed a Russian fleet, and declared war on Russia. The Japanese won many land and sea battles during the Russo-Japanese war, which ended when both sides signed a peace treaty the following year. In 1910, Korea became a Japanese territory.

By the time the Meiji era came to an end in 1912, with the death of Emperor Meiji, Japan was already established as a world power.

War for Korea

During the Meiji period, Japan wanted to extend its territories. In 1894-5 its forces crushed the Chinese navy and gained control of Taiwan. Here you can see a Chinese ship sinking during the battle of Yalu in 1894.

△Under Meiji rule, Japan's industrialization was accelerated, using Western technology. This included the establishment of a national railway system.

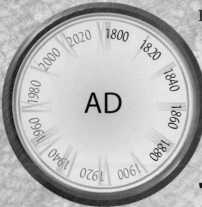

AD

During the 1700s, the slave trade brought misery to thousands of Africans, who were transported across the Atlantic Ocean and forced to work as slaves on plantations in the Americas. This trade also brought huge wealth to those who ran it – the shipbuilders, shipowners, merchants, and traders.

The Scramble for Africa

Many people began to condemn the slave trade and to call for it to be abolished. The slave trade came to an end in the British Empire in 1807, and slavery was finally abolished within the empire in 1833. Slavery continued elsewhere, however. It did not come to an end in the United States until after the American Civil War in 1865. It continued in Brazil until 1889.

Into Africa

In 1822, Liberia was founded on the coast of West Africa by freed slaves. Many of these slaves came from the United States. There were others that came from slave ships that were captured by the British navy after the abolition of the slave trade.

British slave trade abolished.	1807
Liberia founded on coast of West Africa as a country for freed slaves.	1822
Abolition of slavery in British Empire.	1833
King Leopold II of Belgium lays claim to Congo region.	1880
Britain takes control of Egypt and Suez Canal.	1882
Conference in Berlin divides Africa among European countries.	1884
Italians take control of Eritrea.	1890
French take control of Mali.	1893

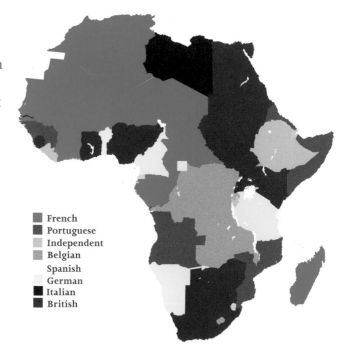

▷ In the late 1880s, the continent of Africa, with the exception of Ethiopia and Liberia, was divided up between the European nations of Belgium, Britain, France, Germany, Italy, Portugal, and Spain.

French
Portuguese
Independent
Belgian
Spanish
German
Italian
British

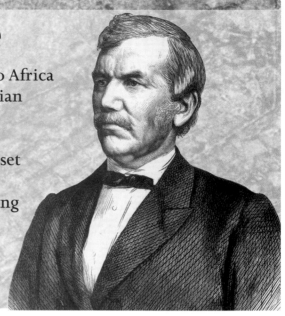

David Livingstone

Livingstone first went to Africa in 1841 to join a Christian missionary station in Bechuanaland (modern Botswana). In 1853, he set out on the first of three great expeditions, walking from Africa's west coast across to the Indian Ocean in the east.

△ The anti-slavery movement was strongest in Britain and the United States. After the abolition of slavery, many abolitionist speakers, shown here, joined the struggle to gain equal rights for black people.

△ While slavery was abolished throughout the British Empire, it continued in the US. Some slaves worked as servants in the homes of their owners. They often enjoyed better living conditions and more privileges.

Elsewhere in Africa, European adventurers were beginning to explore the interior of the continent. Although Europeans had established trading bases around the African coastline, very little was known about the empires and people of Africa. In 1788, an association was formed in London to encourage British exploration and trade in Africa. In the 1800s, the Industrial Revolution had resulted in increasing European interest in Africa as a source of cheap raw materials and as a market for manufactured goods.

Many British explorers set out to explore Africa along its rivers. They included Mungo Park, Richard Burton, and John Speke. Probably the most famous of all the expeditions was led by David Livingstone, who set out to look for the source of the River Nile. After being out of contact for almost three years, Livingstone was "found" by the American journalist Henry Stanley. Stanley went on to organize expeditions along the Congo River on behalf of the king of Belgium, who wanted to establish an overseas empire.

Dividing Africa

In the late 1800s, other European countries also began to lay claim to large areas of Africa. In 1884, a conference was held by the European nations in Berlin, Germany, to decide how Africa should be divided between them. No African representatives were present at the conference. By 1914, the only two countries on the African continent that still remained independent were Liberia and Ethiopia.

△ This is a typical colonists' hat. Colonists argued over each other's claims to the colonies. Yet colonial rule lasted for fewer than 100 years in most countries.

At the beginning of the 1800s, the population of Ireland stood at about five million. In the first 40 years of the century, the population increased to about eight million. Many people lived in extreme poverty.

Famine in Ireland

In 1845, a fungus affected the vital potato crop in southern England. It soon spread to Ireland, and in an unusually cold and wet year, the fungus quickly swept across the entire country.

Famine strikes

With the failure of the potato crop, people began to die in the thousands either from hunger or disease. In 1845, British Prime Minister Sir Robert Peel organized relief for the poorest people, so they could afford to buy inexpensive corn imported from the United States. It helped to prevent many people from starving to death. But when Peel resigned, the new government did little to assist the people of Ireland, limiting its help to building extra workhouses and opening up soup kitchens.

Potato crop fails in southern England. Fungus spreads to Ireland.	1845
Famine in Ireland kills about one million people. Many thousands emigrate.	1845–1849
Fenian Brotherhood formed in U.S.	1858
Home Rule movement founded by Isaac Butt.	1870
Charles Parnell becomes leader of Home Rule movement.	1878
First Home Rule Bill is defeated. Gladstone forced to resign.	1886
Second Home Rule Bill defeated by the House of Lords.	1893

△ Poor Irish people relied on potatoes as their main source of food. Between 1845 and 1849, an estimated one million people in Ireland died, either from starvation or disease.

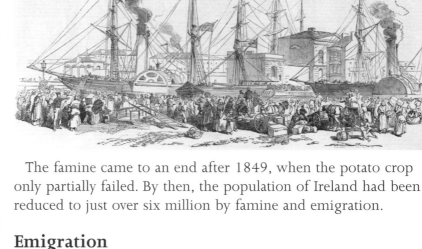

▷ Irish emigrants wait to board a ship taking them to the United States. They were often forced to endure appalling conditions during the long voyage. One in nine emigrants from Cork, in Ireland, died before they reached their destination.

The famine came to an end after 1849, when the potato crop only partially failed. By then, the population of Ireland had been reduced to just over six million by famine and emigration.

Emigration

Many thousands of Irish people decided that their only escape from the great hunger caused by the famine was emigration. Over half a million people emigrated across the Atlantic to the United States between 1845 and 1849.

Many Irish people felt great bitterness towards the British government once the famine was over. This led to the founding of organizations, such as the Fenian Brotherhood in the U.S., which were prepared to fight for the establishment of an Irish republic, completely separate from Britain.

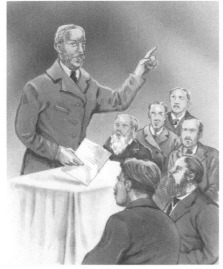

△ Irish politician Charles Parnell addresses an audience in support of Home Rule. He became leader of the Home Rule Party in the British parliament and fought tirelessly for his beliefs. Parnell was even imprisoned by the British for a time.

Home Rule

In 1870, a movement calling for Home Rule was founded in Ireland. Supporters of Home Rule wanted a separate parliament to deal with Irish affairs in Dublin. Although the British government was forced to introduce many reforms, two bills to introduce Home Rule were defeated in parliament in the 1880s and 1890s.

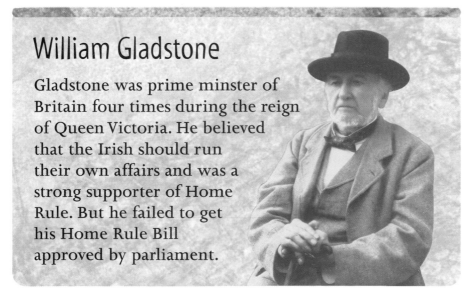

William Gladstone

Gladstone was prime minster of Britain four times during the reign of Queen Victoria. He believed that the Irish should run their own affairs and was a strong supporter of Home Rule. But he failed to get his Home Rule Bill approved by parliament.

△ When Ireland's potato crop failed, people dug up their crops only to find them rotting in the ground. Others picked what looked like sound potatoes, but they simply went rotten later on.

31

AD

When Queen Victoria came to the throne in 1837, Great Britain was one of the wealthiest and most powerful countries in the world. Much of Britain's wealth came from its colonies, which provided sources of inexpensive raw materials and markets for British manufactured goods.

The British Empire

Britain began to acquire its overseas colonies during the 1600s. Although it lost the colonies in America in 1783, British influence continued to be extended in other parts of the world.

Britain takes control of Cape Colony in southern Africa.	1806
Start of reign of Queen Victoria.	1837
Revolt against British in India ends in terrible bloodshed.	1857–1858
End of rule of East India Company. British government takes control.	1858
Suez Canal is opened.	1869
Queen Victoria becomes empress of India.	1877
First Boer War ends with British defeat.	1880–1881
Second Boer War – Boers are forced to surrender.	1889–1902

Captain James Cook claimed parts of Australia and New Zealand in the 1770s. The first convicts were sent to Australia in 1788 because Britain was using the new land as a prison colony. In 1801, the Act of Union made Ireland part of the United Kingdom of Great Britain and Ireland. At the end of the Napoleonic Wars, Britain kept control of some of the colonies it had seized during the fighting.

India

The British set up their first trading post in India in 1612 and by the end of the 1600s had bases at Madras, Bombay, and Calcutta. These trading stations were run by the East India Company. In 1757, there was an uprising against the British in Calcutta but they eventually emerged victorious. This date marks the beginning of the British Empire in India.

The British gradually extended their power across India and trade flourished. One of the exports to India was cotton

△ Resentment to British rule boiled over in 1857, when Indian troops mutinied and marched on Delhi. The rebellion spread quickly across India, and thousands died in the fighting.

Suez Canal

Although Britain had played no part in building the Suez Canal in Egypt, it benefited greatly when the canal opened in 1869. The new 118-mile-long waterway shortened the route from Britain to India by around 6,000 miles.

△ *During Queen Victoria's long reign, lasting 63 years, Britain's empire expanded greatly. At its largest, the British Empire accounted for one-fourth of the world's population.*

cloth, produced inexpensively in British factories. However, local Indian producers could not compete with the British cloth and many went out of business.

In 1857, Indian soldiers mutinied against British control. By the following year, the rebellion had been put down and the British had regained control. But the East India Company's rule came to an end in 1858, and the British government took over running India. Queen Victoria was crowned empress of India in 1877.

The Boers

In southern Africa, Cape Colony came under British rule in 1806. However, the area was already home to the Boers – descendants of Dutch settlers. To escape British control, thousands of Boers undertook a journey northward in the 1830s, known as the "Great Trek." They founded two Boer states: the Orange Free State and the Transvaal. When the British tried to increase their power in southern Africa, the two sides went to war. The first Boer War (1880–1881) ended with a British defeat.

In 1886, major gold deposits were discovered in Witwatersrand in the Transvaal. Britain feared the growing power and wealth of the Boer states, and war broke out again in 1899. The Boers were finally forced to surrender in 1902.

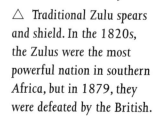

△ *Traditional Zulu spears and shield. In the 1820s, the Zulus were the most powerful nation in southern Africa, but in 1879, they were defeated by the British.*

> Move [the statue of] Queen Anne? Most certainly not! Why it might some day be suggested that *my* statue should be moved, which I should much dislike.
> **QUEEN VICTORIA, 1887**

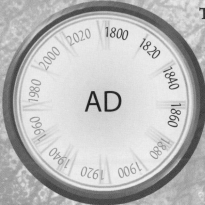

AD

The early settlement of North America by Europeans was along the east coast. However, the Appalachian Mountains formed a natural barrier, initially preventing expansion farther west. In 1783, after the American Revolution, the United States took control of land west of the Appalachian Mountains as far as the Mississippi River, and pioneers began to settle in the area.

Pioneers in the U.S.

President Jefferson makes Louisiana Purchase, almost doubling size of the U.S.	1803
Journey of Lewis and Clark to the west.	1804–1805
Start of great migration westward on California and Oregon trails.	1840s
Southern Oregon given to U.S. by Britain.	1846
Mexican War fought between U.S. and Mexico ends with victory for U.S.	1846–1848
Mormons begin their settlement of Utah.	1847
Gold discovered in California, setting off Gold Rush.	1848
U.S. government begins policy of "concentration" for Native Americans.	1851

Following the purchase of Louisiana from France in 1803, President Jefferson had sent out an expedition to find out more about his new territories. The expedition leaders, Meriwether Lewis and William Clark, were the first of the many explorers and traders who started to travel westward, opening up routes called trails.

The Oregon and California trails

The first pioneers to go west were lured by tales of rich farmland on the far side of the Rocky Mountains. From the 1840s onward, large

△ The bolder pioneers made their way westward in long trains of covered wagons. They crossed the vast expanse of treeless plains to the Rocky Mountains, drawn by stories of fertile farmland and abundant forests.

△ As the news of the discovery of gold spread, people from all over the world poured into California. However, very few actually made their fortunes.

Custer's last stand

At the battle of the Little Bighorn in June 1876, Lieutenant Colonel George Custer and his unit of around 200 soldiers were killed by Sioux and Cheyenne Indians. The battle became known as "Custer's last stand."

△ By 1835, around 100 miles of railway track were in operation in the United States. The US government had granted over 200 railroad charters.

△ Cowboys would drive huge herds of cattle across the plains on long trail drives. They took the cattle from the ranches in the west to railway stations to be shipped to the towns of the east.

numbers of people made the hazardous journey westward. Many traveled across the continent along the 1,990 mile Oregon Trail. It started in Independence, Missouri, and ended in the Columbia River region of Oregon. An alternative trail, the California Trail, followed the same route until it branched southward west of the Rocky Mountains, ending in the Sacramento Valley.

The pioneers traveled in wagons known as "prairie schooners" because their white canvas tops looked like sails. Settlers moved along the trail in groups for safety and for companionship, and there could be up to 100 wagons in a single wagon train. Although the greatest fear for pioneers was attack from Native Americans, the major killer was actually disease, and many pioneers died on the trails.

The gold rush

In 1848, James Marshall discovered gold in the America River at Sutter's Mill in California. Gold seekers began to come from all over the world, traveling by ship to San Francisco. Others walked across the American continent. Many died before they even reached California.

Native Americans on the move

As more people settled in the West, Native American ways of life were destroyed. In 1860, there were at least two million buffalo, on which the Native Americans relied, roaming across the Great Plains. White hunters began to destroy the large herds, and within 25 years, the number of buffalo had dropped drastically to about 2,000. Many Native Americans fought for their land and traditions, but they were usually no match for the well-equipped soldiers of the American government.

AD

During the 1800s and the beginning of the 1900s, many important discoveries were made in a wide range of scientific fields – from evolution to electricity, and from medicine to communications

Science and Technology

Pioneering work was done by people such as Charles Darwin, Thomas A. Edison, Alexander Graham Bell, and Guglielmo Marconi, changing the way people thought and lived in many parts of the world.

Steamship Clermont makes first trip on the Hudson River	1807
British engineer George Stephenson builds steam locomotive Rocket.	1829
Darwin's voyage on the Beagle.	1831–1836
Steamship Sirius starts first regular transatlantic steam-powered service.	1838
Great Britain is first propeller-driven ship to cross the Atlantic.	1845
Publication of Darwin's The Origin of Species.	1859
Great Eastern lays first successful underwater telegraph line across Atlantic.	1866
Alexander Graham Bell develops first telephone.	1876
Guglielmo Marconi develops wireless telegraphy.	1895

Steam power

The importance of steam power was already well established by the early 1800s, but it was not until 1829 that the British engineer George Stephenson built the first practical steam locomotive, the Rocket. The opening of the Liverpool to Manchester railway in northwest England in the following year marked the beginning of the railway age.

Steam was also used to power ships. The first regular transatlantic steam-powered service began in 1838 by the steamship Sirius. It had side wheels to push it through the water. The next major development in sea travel was the development of the screw propeller. The Great Britain, built by Isambard Kingdom Brunel, was the first propeller-driven ship to cross the Atlantic, in 1845.

Scientific expeditions

Of the scientific expeditions undertaken during the 1800s, one of the most famous was the voyage made by Charles Darwin on the HMS Beagle.

△ From the observations made on his 37,000 mile journey on board the Beagle, Darwin began to piece together his theory of evolution. It caused a storm of controversy when it was first published, although many people came to accept it.

△ *One of the first electric street lamps. American Thomas Edison invented the first working electric lamp in 1879. In the late 1800s, electric lamps began to replace gas ones.*

Samuel Morse

In 1840, the American inventor Samuel F. B. Morse launched a code based on dots, dashes, and spaces. Known as the Morse code, it speeded up the sending of messages through the telegraph.

From 1831 to 1836, the naval survey ship sailed around the world. Darwin collected plant and animal specimens for scientific institutions in Britain. From his observations he, developed his theory of evolution, published in 1859. It stated that all living things evolved from ancestors by a process of natural selection.

Communications

The first truly rapid system for communicating between one place and another was the electric telegraph, which sent messages along wires. Soon most major cities were linked by telegraph, and in 1866, the first successful underwater telegraph line was laid across the Atlantic Ocean by the *Great Eastern*.

In 1876, a Scottish inventor, Alexander Graham Bell, made the first telephone. For the first time it was possible to transmit the human voice along a wire link. The next major breakthrough in communications was to send information without wires. In 1895, an Italian inventor, Guglielmo Marconi, developed wireless telegraphy, which made use of invisible radio waves to carry information. In 1906, a Canadian, Reginald A. Fessenden, made the first broadcast, transmitting speech and music to his astonished listeners.

△ *A new kind of bicycle called the penny farthing appeared in the 1860s. It had a very large front wheel and a smaller back wheel.*

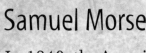

"We must, however, acknowledge, as it seems to me, that man with all his noble qualities, ... still bears in his bodily frame the indelible stamp of his lowly origin.
CHARLES DARWIN (1809–1882)

The Manchus (from Manchuria) ruled China for more than 250 years, from 1644 until 1912. This time is known as the Qing dynasty.

Rebellion in China

In the early part of Manchu reign, China was peaceful and prosperous. The population increased, and new, improved crops were introduced. Trade flourished, and China exported large amounts of tea and silk to countries in Europe. However, like rulers before them, the Manchus were careful to restrict imports from Europe. Foreign traders were allowed to do business in only one Chinese port, Guangzhou, and they had to pay for Chinese goods only in silver or gold.

The Opium Wars

In the early 1800s, British merchants began to trade opium illegally from India to China. Despite the fact that the addictive dangers of opium were well known, the British government backed the merchants. They wanted to force China to accept more open trade.

The first Opium War broke out in 1839, ending with the Treaty of Nanjing in 1842. Under the terms of this treaty, Hong Kong became a British colony and more Chinese ports were opened up to European trade. A second Opium War (1856–1860) extended the trading rights of European nations in China.

First Opium War fought between China and Britain.	1839–1842
Taiping Rebellion against Qing dynasty ends in terrible bloodshed.	1851–1864
Second Opium War ends with more trading rights for Britain.	1856–1860
War between China and Japan results in loss of Taiwan to Japan.	1894–1895
Boxer Rebellion. Attacks on westerners and Chinese Christians.	1900
Revolution in China.	1911
End of the Qing dynasty.	1912

△ The Boxers were one of a number of Chinese secret societies strongly opposed to the spreading influence of Western and Christian ideas in China.

▷ Under the Qing dynasty, Guangzhou was the only Chinese port that Western ships could use. Traders were strictly controlled and were only allowed access to a small area of the port.

△ The first Opium War began when Chinese officials seized 20,000 chests of opium in Guangzhou. It lasted from 1839 until a treaty was signed in 1842.

Uprising and rebellion

By the end of the 1700s, China's population was growing so fast that food production could not keep up. There was widespread corruption and any attempts to modernize were met with opposition from bureacrats and officials. There was a series of rebellions against Manchu rule in the 1800s, which helped to weaken the Qing dynasty. The Taiping Rebellion lasted for 14 years, and thousands of people died in these uprisings. In 1894–1895, China fought a war against Japan which resulted in the loss of the territory of Taiwan.

After the treaties that ended the Opium Wars, Western ideas began to spread in China. Some Chinese people opposed Western influences, and in 1900, the Boxer Rebellion broke out. Many Europeans were killed, but a combined European army eventually put down the rebellion.

After 1900, revolutionary groups began to oppose the Manchu rulers. The Manchus started to reform the government – but it was too late. In October 1911, there was a revolution and the last emperor was forced to abdicate. China had become a republic.

Hong Kong

The skyline of modern Hong Kong. The island of Hong Kong came under British control in 1842, and Britain later gained part of the nearby Kowloon Peninsula. Control of Hong Kong passed back to the Chinese government in 1997.

△ Under Manchu rule, all Chinese males had to follow the tradition of wearing their hair in a pigtail. It was seen as a sign of loyalty to the Qing dynasty.

The women's movement had its roots in the late 1700s and early 1800s. Changes such as the American and French revolutions promoted ideas of "equality" and "liberty," yet women were not permitted to vote, and most had limited access to education.

The Women's Movement

Mary Wollstonecraft's A Vindication of the Rights of Women.	1792
First Women's Rights Convention held in Seneca Falls, New York.	1848
Wyoming becomes first US state to grant women the right to vote.	1890
New Zealand is first country in the world to allow women to vote in elections.	1893
In Britain, Emmeline Pankhurst founds the WSPU.	1903
Suffragette Emily Davison throws herself beneath the king's horse at a race.	1913
Women over 30 given the vote in Britain.	1918
All women over 21 given the vote in Britain.	1928

In 1792, a British writer named Mary Wollstonecraft published *A Vindication of the Rights of Women*, setting out her belief in equal rights for men and women. This idea took hold during the 1800s, and many women began to campaign for reform.

Reform in the U.S.

The campaign for women's rights in the United States developed from the fight against slavery. The first Women's Rights Convention was held in Seneca Falls, New York, in 1848, organized by Lucretia Mott and Elizabeth Cady Stanton. Stanton declared that "all men and women are created equal" and called for reform in the laws concerning suffrage (the right to vote), marriage, and ownership of property. Stanton later teamed up with another reformer called Susan B. Anthony, and they traveled all over North America giving lectures and speaking at rallies in support of women's rights.

In 1890, Wyoming became the first state to grant women the right to vote. But it was to be another 30 years, not until 1920, before women's suffrage was extended to all the states.

△ Emmeline Pankhurst, founder of the WSPU, is arrested. She died a month after British women gained equal voting rights.

△ The suffragettes engaged in many different forms of protest, from interrupting public meetings by shouting slogans to chaining themselves to railings outside the residence of the British prime minister.

In prison

In Britain, the suffragette campaigners often went on hunger strikes when imprisoned for their actions. The authorities did not want the suffragettes to die and arouse public sympathy, so they fed the women by force.

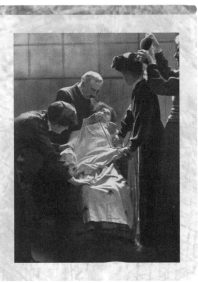

Suffragettes

In 1893, New Zealand became the first country in the world to allow women to vote in national elections. Australia followed suit in 1903 and Finland in 1906. In other parts of the world, however, women were engaged in a bitter and often violent battle for the right to vote. In Britain, Emmeline Pankhurst founded the Women's Social and Political Union (WSPU) in 1903. The WSPU believed in actions rather than words, and many of its members, known as suffragettes, were arrested and imprisoned. In 1913, a suffragette called Emily Davison was killed when she threw herself beneath the king's horse at a race. Women over 30 were finally given the vote in 1918, after World War I. The right to vote was extended to all women over the age of 21 in 1928.

Just as in Britain, World War I was a turning-point in many countries for the women's movement. During the war, women had filled the places of the men who had gone off to fight, working in industries such as munitions factories, on farms as laborers, and in the mines. After the end of the war, equal voting rights were introduced in Canada (1918), Austria, Czechoslovakia, Germany, and Poland (1919), and in 1920 in Hungary and the United States.

△ During wartime women were brought in to fill the jobs of those men that had gone to fight. These posters emphasized the important role women had to play.

> The divine right of husbands, like the divine right of kings, may, it is hoped, in this enlightened age, be contested without danger.
> ## MARY WOLLSTONECRAFT (1759–1797)
> *Wollstonecraft's book* A Vindication of the Rights of Women, *which she wrote in 1792, called for equal rights for women.*

AD

The events of the Industrial Revolution brought great changes to towns and cities in Britain, and then across Europe and North America. British cities such as Birmingham, Manchester, Leeds, and Liverpool became important industrial centers, and their populations expanded rapidly.

Urban Development

First law concerning public health passed in England.	1848
Much of Paris redesigned and rebuilt.	1851–1870
Invention of Bessemer process makes use of steel in construction.	1856
First skyscraper, Home Insurance Building in Chicago, completed.	1885
Construction of Eiffel Tower for Paris Exhibition.	1889
Empire State Building constructed in New York City.	1931

People needed to live close to their workplace, so large numbers of houses were built to accommodate this new class of industrial worker. The speed with which many towns and cities expanded led to problems with overcrowded, dirty, and unsanitary housing.

Slum conditions

Many workers were forced to live in slum conditions. Worse, the new factories created pollution that often contaminated both water supplies and the air. Early industrial cities were disease-ridden places with very high death rates. Cholera, in particular, killed both rich and poor, and it claimed more than 140,000 people in Britain in four epidemics from 1831 to 1866. It was not until the mid-1800s in Britain that measures began to be taken to improve sanitation and health, for example by installing proper sewerage systems.

The increase in city populations was dramatic during the 1800s. London's

▷ The new factories in Britain's industrial cities and towns created pollution, often contaminating water supplies and the surrounding air. This pollution, and the poor housing conditions, led to the spread of disease.

△ The families of many workers lived in appalling slum conditions in the cities, often without clean water and proper sewage facilities.

Skyscrapers

Land prices in American cities were so high that people began to build upward. The first "skyscraper," the ten-story Home Insurance Building in Chicago, was completed in 1885.

population jumped from just under one million at the beginning of the century to over two million in 1840. Chicago increased in population from about 4,000 in 1840 to over one million people only 50 years later.

Ideal cities

Some people were appalled by the conditions in industrial cities. Writers such as Charles Dickens exposed the desperation of the poor in London in many of his novels. Some reformers tried to show how workers could, and should, be treated. One such reformer was a British industrialist named Robert Owen. He drew up plans for an "ideal city," showing how the houses, factories, shops, and other buildings should be arranged. Sadly, his plans were not taken seriously by the authorities.

Improvements

Improvements came as governments realized that more control was needed over the design and position of buildings in cities. Public services such as clean water supplies, sewage, gas and electric lighting, and public transport were also put in place.

In some places, parts of the old city were swept away to be replaced by radical new designs. This happened in Paris, where much of the medieval center was replaced by the ambitious plans of Baron Haussmann. Haussmann opened up 60 miles of new streets in the center of Paris, creating some of the spacious avenues for which Paris is still famous.

In cities such as New York and Chicago, the first skyscrapers appeared, built around a framework of strong, light steel.

△ Life in the industrial centers revolved around the mines, mills, and factories where people worked.

The opening years of the 20th century saw rivalry growing between the nations of Europe. Countries such as Britain and France controlled vast colonies overseas – in Africa and Southeast Asia – giving them both power and wealth.

Revolutions and Wars

Germany, which had become a united country in 1871, wanted to expand its territory and began to build up its military power. As countries became increasingly suspicious of each other, they entered into alliances – promising to help each other in the event of attack. In 1882, Germany, Austria-Hungary, and Italy formed the Triple Alliance. In 1904, Britain announced its friendly relations with France, and in 1907, they were joined by Russia to form the Triple Entente. It was these tensions and suspicions that led to the outbreak of World War I in 1914.

Conflict and unrest

In Russia, many years of strikes and protests came to a head in 1905, when workers went to the palace of the tsar, Nicholas II, in St. Petersburg to ask for reforms. Troops fired on the unarmed crowd, sparking a revolution which was put down by the government. A series

of disastrous campaigns in World War I, rising unemployment, and constant food shortages led to the successful overthrow of the tsar's regime in 1917 and the installation of a new communist government in Russia.

In Ireland, the issue of Home Rule, the Irish governing themselves, was the cause of violent protest, which finally erupted into civil war in 1921. An uneasy peace was negotiated in 1923, but the Irish problem was to continue throughout the century.

The Great Depression

A disastrous stock market crash in 1929 in the United States left many people penniless overnight. The effects of the Wall Street Crash were felt all over the world. Many countries in Europe were hard hit because they had borrowed money from the U.S. at the end of World War I. Throughout the 1930s, unemployment soared and trade slumped in a period known as the Great Depression.

In Germany and Italy, Fascist governments swept to power in the 1920s and 1930s. The Fascist leaders Benito Mussolini and Adolf Hitler promised to make their countries strong and successful once more. In 1939, after a bitter civil war, Spain also had a Fascist government. In the same year, Germany invaded Poland, marking the beginning of World War II.

AD

In 1801, the grandson of Catherine the Great, Alexander I, became tsar (emperor) of Russia. Alexander had grand plans to introduce reform to his vast country, for example a program of building schools and the founding of new universities.

Revolution in Russia

Alexander I, becomes tsar of Russia.	1801
Russian army defeated by French at battle of Austerlitz.	1805
French retreat from Moscow.	1812
Nicholas I becomes tsar. Decembrist revolt.	1825
Crimean War.	1853–1856
Alexander II begins series of reforms.	1855
Serfs given freedom.	1861
Alexander II killed by terrorist bomb. His son Alexander III succeeds.	1881
Nicholas II becomes last tsar.	1894
Revolution put down by government troops.	1905
Russian Revolution.	1917

In 1805, the armies of the French emperor, Napoleon Bonaparte defeated a combined Russian and Austrian force at the battle of Austerlitz in Moravia. In 1812, French armies invaded Russia and advanced as far as Moscow. The French found the city deserted, and soon afterward, it was almost completely destroyed by fire.

Reform and modernization

At the end of the Napoleonic Wars, Russia emerged as a major European power. During the reign of Nicholas I, Russian armies helped to quell revolutions in Poland and Hungary, and gained territory for Russia around the Black Sea. But during the Crimean War, Russia was humiliated by its defeat at the hands of a combined French and British force.

Nicholas I remained deeply opposed to any change. He died in 1855 and was succeeded by his son, Alexander II. Shocked by the outcome of the Crimean War, the new tsar was determined to modernize Russia. He oversaw a massive program of reform, including railway building and the reorganization of local government and the legal system. Probably his most important action

△ In November 1917, armed workers, soldiers, and sailors, led by the Bolshevik revolutionaries, took up positions in the city of Petrograd (St. Petersburg). They stormed the Winter Palace, the headquarters of Russia's provisional government, and seized power.

△ *Nicholas II and his family. Imprisoned by the Bolsheviks in 1917, they were most likely shot the following year.*

V. I. Lenin

Lenin was one of the leaders of the failed rebellion in 1905. He was forced into exile but returned to Russia in 1917 when the tsar was overthrown. He led the Bolsheviks to victory in the revolution of 1917.

was to abolish serfdom. In 1861, serfs were given their freedom and land was distributed between them.

The Russian Revolution

The last tsar, Nicholas II, ruled from 1894 until his abdication in 1917. In the early years of his reign, there was increasing discontent among ordinary Russians. Many people, including the Bolshevik leader Vladimir Illyich (V. I.) Lenin, followed the teachings of Karl Marx, the founder of communism. In 1905, this discontent boiled over when troops fired on thousands of striking workers outside the tsar's Winter Palace in St. Petersburg. The rebellion was quickly put down, but hundreds of workers were killed and wounded.

During World War I, Russia was allied with France and Great Britain. The Russian armies suffered defeats on the Eastern Front, and the Russian economy began to collapse. In early 1917, riots broke out again – and this time the troops supported the rioters. Nicholas II abdicated, and a provisional government was put in place. Later in 1917, the Bolsheviks seized power and formed a new government with Lenin at its head. The events of 1917 are known as the Russian Revolution.

△ *The red flag of the Bolshevik revolutionaries. Later, the symbols of a hammer and a sickle (to represent workers and peasants) and a star were added to create the official Communist Party flag.*

Communism is Soviet power plus the electrification of the whole country.
VLADIMIR ILLYICH LENIN, DECEMBER 1920

INDEX